Bowie

Bowie
An Illustrated Life

María Hesse   Fran Ruiz

Translated from the Spanish by Ned Sublette

University of Texas Press ⌁ Austin

The verse on page 22, "Life is a cigarette," is a translation from
"Chants Andalous" by Manuel Machado y Ruiz, a poem that could
have inspired the first verse of the song "Rock and Roll Suicide."

First edition: April 2018
Illustrations © 2018 by María Hesse
Text © 2018 by Fran Ruiz
© 2018 for the Spanish-language edition throughout the world:
Penguin Random House Grupo Editorial, S.A.U.
Travessera de Gràcia, 47-49. 08021 Barcelona

First University of Texas Press edition, 2019
English translation © 2019 by Ned Sublette
All rights reserved
Printed in China

Requests for permission to reproduce material from
this work should be sent to:
Permissions
University of Texas Press
P.O. Box 7819
Austin, TX 78713-7819
utpress.utexas.edu/rp-form

♾ The paper used in this book meets the minimum requirements of
ANSI/NISO Z39.48-1992 (R1997) (Permanence of Paper).

Library of Congress Cataloging-in-Publication Data

Names: Hesse, Maria, author. | Ruiz, Fran, author.
Title: Bowie : an illustrated life / Maria Hesse, Fran Ruiz ; translated from
the Spanish by Ned Sublette.
Other titles: Bowie, una biografia. English
Description: First University of Texas Press edition, 2019. | Austin :
University of Texas Press, 2019. | Includes bibliographical references.
Identifiers: LCCN 2018052867
        ISBN 978-1-4773-1887-4 (cloth : alk. paper)
        ISBN 978-1-4773-1888-1 (library e-book)
        ISBN 978-1-4773-1889-8 (nonlibrary e-book)
Subjects: LCSH: Bowie, David. | Rock musicians—England—Biography.
Classification: LCC ML420.B754 H4813 2019 | DDC 782.42166092
[B] —dc23
LC record available at https://lccn.loc.gov/2018052867

doi:10.7560/318874

For our nieces and nephews: Alicia, Andrea,
Gonzalo, Manuela, and Ramón,
who one day will discover life on Mars.

IF I'VE BEEN AT ALL RESPONSIBLE FOR PEOPLE FINDING
MORE CHARACTERS IN THEMSELVES THAN THEY
ORIGINALLY THOUGHT THEY HAD, THEN I'M PLEASED.

—DAVID BOWIE to Alan Yentob,
in the documentary *Cracked Actor* (1975)

CONTENTS

INTRODUCTION

This book is several things.

First, it's the result of many hours of documentation of one of the most emblematic artists of our time.

Second, it's a re-created biography of someone who resisted talking about himself and, when he did, typically falsified his story.

Third, and above all, it's a display of admiration and affection on the part of two people whose lives have been profoundly influenced by the music and art of David Bowie.

Bowie was a master of artifice and of masking. To tell his story, we decided to use the same lens. In his work our hero taught us that to show things through a single prism, as honest as that might seem, might explain less than a fragmented, ambiguous version. Because of that, and because we're aware that a biography is inevitably a work of fiction, we decided to mix passages of Bowie's real life with fantastical elements. Doing this, we hope to get closer to the reality of one of the most interesting and enigmatic people we never met: playing at what David Robert Jones might have thought and felt at different moments of his life. To play is to try to intuit. This is not deceit.

We hope you enjoy this book and that it helps you get to know Bowie better. When you finish, maybe you'll want to listen to one of his albums. You could start with *Hunky Dory* or *Station to Station*. We've been enjoying them for years.

David Bowie

I THINK MY THEMES HAVE ALWAYS BEEN THE CONCEPTS OF ISOLATION AND ALIENATION.

I arrive on planet Earth in 1947. The Joneses, a cold and formal family, welcome me into their arms and raise me on the outskirts of London.

At the age of fifteen a meteorite hits me in the left eye, transforming it forever. I begin to be as strange on the outside as I feel inside.

1963

Dark spirits possess my dear half-brother, Terry, provoking schizophrenia in him for the rest of his days.

1970

I marry Angie Barnett, an attractive and bisexual American. We share a thirst for fame and success, and sometimes we share our lovers.

1971

My son, Duncan Zowie Haywood Jones, is born. I feel like something important is about to happen.

1972

I present to the world the alien who lives in me: Ziggy Stardust. I achieve the musical renown I'd dreamed of. I never felt so sexy and powerful.

1974

Attracted by bright lights and black music, I move to the United States, where I consume large quantities of cocaine.

1977

I leave Los Angeles to kick my coke habit and get rid of demon spirits. I move to Berlin with my friend Iggy Pop.

1980

I divorce Angie. I never speak to her again.

1983

I release the album *Let's Dance*, which makes me fabulously wealthy. I become a movie star.

1985

Overwhelmed by his schizophrenia, my half-brother, Terry, commits suicide. I decide not to attend the funeral.

1992

I marry Iman Mohamed Abdulmajid. At last I feel calm inside.

2000

Our daughter, Alexandria Zahra Jones, is born. I decide to be the best possible dad.

2004

I have a heart attack during a concert in Germany. I never go back on the road, and my health never fully recovers.

2016

My stay in this world reaches its end. I become dust and stars once again.

ABSOLUTE BEGINNERS

I'm Major Tom. I'm Ziggy Stardust. I'm the Thin White Duke. I'm an extraterrestrial. I'm the king of the goblins. I'm the Elephant Man. I'm "the dying man who can't die." I'm the replicant's brother. I'm Lazarus. I'm the man who carries the burden of a black star on his shoulders. I'm the black star as well. I'm everything you can't imagine.

BY THE TIME YOU THINK YOU'VE GLIMPSED WHAT'S HIDING BEHIND MY SILHOUETTE, I'LL HAVE TRANSFORMED INTO SOMETHING ELSE.

My name is David Robert Haywood Jones. I decided to come into the world on a January 8 because Elvis did. That night, a brilliant sphere fell on 40 Stansfield Road, London. The neighbors paid it no mind. It was a ghostly reminder of the many missiles that rained on the East End during the Second World War, leaving in ruins the area around the street where I was born.

My father, Haywood Stenton Jones, was a public relations man for a charity for children. A loving man with a tendency toward sadness, he adored new technologies, radio and television, and the world of the stage. In his early years he invested in a theater company that went bust. He fought in the war.

My half-brother, Terence Guy Adair Burns, whom we called Terry and who was ten years older than me, was the result of an affair my mother had with one James Rosenburg. It was all the same to me. I loved him a lot. Terry helped me discover American literature, R&B, and jazz. Thanks to those sparks, I became who I am.

My mother, Margaret Burns, Peggy, sold concessions at the movie theater. She had wanted to dedicate herself to singing, but her family obligations prevented her from doing it. Her sisters, Nora, Una, and Vivienne, had mental problems, and her mother (my grandmother) was considered "mad." My mother could be cold and distant if the subject came up.

Me. When I arrived, the midwife said to my mother:

"THIS CHILD HAS BEEN ON EARTH BEFORE."

I have to say that my parents worked hard for Terry and me. We didn't lack for anything. But life in Bromley was boring. Everything was brown or gray, so we had to use our imagination to entertain ourselves. We played in the street among the ruins left by the German bombers and looked for secrets in the abandoned buildings.

It was easier for me to escape the tedium because I wasn't alone.

Many nights the four Joneses would get together around the record player to listen to music. I loved those moments. Then our parents would send us to bed, while they stayed up watching the telly. That was how I furtively discovered the science fiction series *The Quatermass Experiment*. Those space beings captured on screen filled me with fear and fascination. One of them (Z) lived in the house next door, 38 Stansfield Road. It was a secret between him and me.

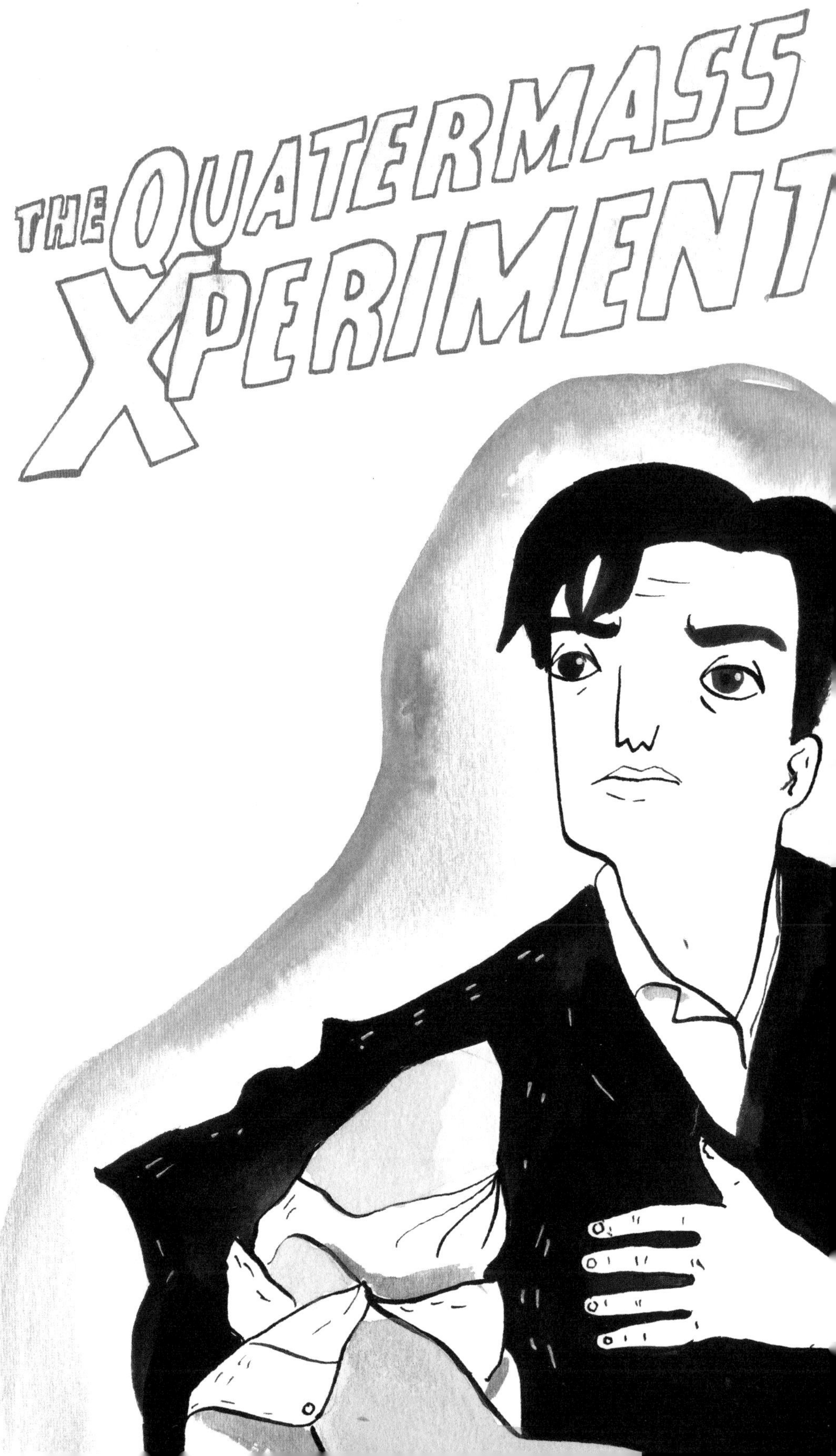
THE QUATERMASS
XPERIMENT

At times he called me from outside my bedroom window. When I went to look, Z drew a door on the window glass with his left ring finger. So I naturally did the same on my window . Then each of us opened his door, and we went out to the street. We walked, staring each other in the eyes, until we met face to face. We stayed like that a few minutes, looking at each other in silence. Then he traced a circle on my forehead, and I did the same on his. The circle felt like an electric tickle, crackling and hot. When the circle began to light up, we each turned around and walked back to our respective houses with our eyes closed. We didn't need to open them. The circles guided us.

This only happened on certain nights, while everyone else was asleep.

One night when Z didn't show up, I dreamed about him. When I woke up the following morning, I found a note under my pillow. The paper was permeated with a fine, glittering dust that stayed on my fingers for years. It said simply:

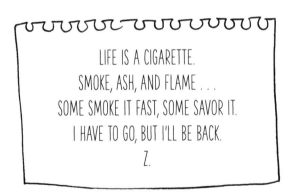

LIFE IS A CIGARETTE.
SMOKE, ASH, AND FLAME . . .
SOME SMOKE IT FAST, SOME SAVOR IT.
I HAVE TO GO, BUT I'LL BE BACK.
Z.

I didn't understand what the hell those words meant. Not then. Neither did I know what made him leave. But I was certain that one day he'd return. And he did. Z was the first talisman that protected me from the existential void.

When I was nine my father brought home a stack of 45 rpm American records. Our machine had only the 78 speed. They sounded strange at that speed, but even so, I loved the music. When I heard Little Richard's "Tutti Frutti," something changed. It revealed the multicolored truth hiding in mundane life. Everything vibrated to the rhythm of the polychromatic energy that emanated from record players, waking a desire in me that I didn't know I had. Then the record stopped, and everything faded again.

BUT THE DESIRE CONTINUED. I INTUITED THAT THE ONLY WAY TO SATIATE IT WAS TO DEDICATE MY LIFE TO MUSIC.

In the church choir I met another kid who wanted to be a musician, George Underwood. Our two passions in common were music and girls. He was taller than I, and people thought he was better looking too. But I dressed better, had a more modern haircut, and knew how to seduce everyone to get what I wanted.

One night we were perched on the roof of my house, watching the stars. I knew that the stars were watching us too. Then something very strange happened: it seemed like a star fell on us and hit me in the left eye. I felt a terrible pain. George and I were very afraid. Since we

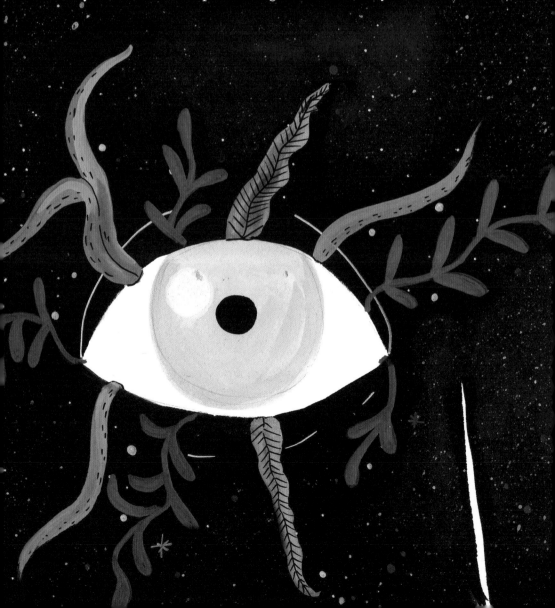

knew no one would believe us if we told the truth, we made up a silly story about him punching me for having stolen his girlfriend. After the accident I couldn't see for weeks. I began to think I wouldn't recover my vision.

AFTER SEVERAL OPERATIONS, MY EYE OPENED AND I COULD SEE AGAIN. NONETHELESS, THE PUPIL REMAINED DILATED ALL MY LIFE. AND ALTHOUGH I WASN'T BLINDED, MY VISION WAS NEVER THE SAME AFTER THAT.

I was fifteen.

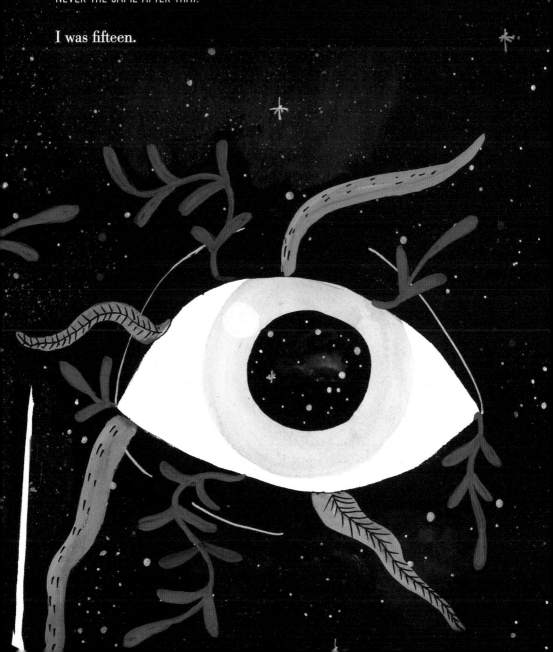

From time to time, Terry brought me into the center of London for concerts and extended sessions looking through bins in record shops. Those were moments of pure liberty and of discovery. Terry was the model I wanted to follow.

I saved up to buy my first instrument, a saxophone, and to pay for some lessons.

I LIKED PLAYING THE SAX BECAUSE IT ALLOWED ME TO BE MY OWN BOSS.

I formed part of two bands with my friend George: George and The Dragons, and The Kon-Rads. But I outgrew them quickly; I needed to be more artistically ambitious and to come with an innovative aesthetic.

With my new group, the King Bees, we managed to play at the birthday party of an electrical appliance tycoon. That's how I met Les Conn, my first manager, who produced my first single: "Louie Louie Go Home/ Liza Jane" by Davie Jones and the King Bees. Then came the Mannish Boys, a rhythm and blues group inspired by Muddy Waters.

When Les Conn got tired of representing a promising but unsuccessful young musician, my career moved over into the hands of Ken Pitt, an educated man who was a publicist and a music-biz veteran. It was Ken who told me to change my name, because Davy Jones was the name of the singer in the Monkees. So I became Bowie, like the hunting knife that cuts in both directions, and together with the Lower Third I released my first single under my new name: "Can't Help Thinking about Me."

None of my early songs was successful. I looked confident on stage, but I was crippled by my insecurities. Did I have the necessary talent to make a name in the music world?

As my adolescence drew to a close, things weren't going well at home. My brother, Terry, had always been a little strange—something I loved about him because I felt the same way. But when he came back from his military service, he started acting *too* strange.

One day we were coming home from a Cream concert at which he had been very nervous when suddenly he threw himself on the ground, muttering that flames were coming up out of the pavement.

I WAS TERRIFIED TO REALIZE WHAT WAS HAPPENING: THE FAMILY CURSE OF SCHIZOPHRENIA HAD GOTTEN HIM.

After that, the arguments between Dad, Mum, and Terry became more frequent. It was unbearable to be there, so I went to live with my manager. Ken's house was a stimulating place to be, full of books and records. We had long conversations. I got a lot of love there:

At last, after much work, I released my first solo LP in 1967: *David Bowie*. I was drunk with happiness to have my dream come true, but it also brought back sharply my uncertainties about whether I could be a success.

LIFTOFF

My first record came and went without grief or glory. I armed myself with patience and kept trying to improve. At the same time, Ken came back from New York with a record for me: *The Velvet Underground & Nico*.

IT WAS RAW, DIRECT ROCK THAT SPOKE OF PEOPLE ON THE EDGE: DRUGGIES, HOMOSEXUALS, PROSTITUTES. I WAS FASCINATED.

My style was lacking that kind of nerve. But the Velvets were a minor group, seemingly inconsequential, and I wanted to go as far as possible.

During this dry spell, Ken encouraged me to try other paths. I started studying to improve my interpretive skills with the brilliant master of mimicry Lindsay Kemp. He taught me that my body could be another artistic tool. Together we put on the mime and music show *Pierrot in Turquoise*.

Lindsay and his boyfriend were prisoners of my seduction. Deep down I couldn't avoid enjoying their jealousy, although I meant them no harm. Nor did I want anyone to be in love with me.

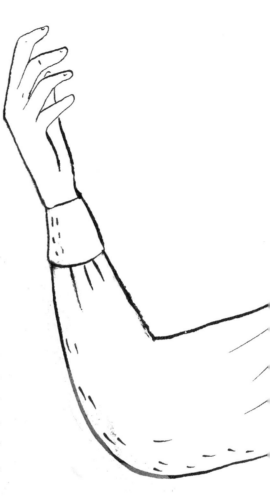

Not even music was enough to satisfy my restless spirit. Between 1967 and 1969 I experimented with Buddhism in Scotland, at the same time as one Leonard Cohen. The lama told me to continue with music, saying:

YOUR ART IS WHAT WILL HELP OTHERS.

I couldn't help but hear in his words the voice of my secret childhood friend.

I left the temple for good, but the ideas of detachment and transience stayed with me, and I never abandoned them.

Through Kemp I met Hermione Farthingale, who was elegant, sophisticated, smart, and upper-class. I could attract anyone I wanted, but I really liked this girl. Together we produced a show called *Feathers*. In summer 1968 we moved to South Kensington.

Being with Hermione calmed my anguish. Her presence reminded me of Z's electric circles. At her side I felt that it was not so urgent to triumph. Things would arrive at the right moment. Unfortunately, we argued often because of jealousy.

For the first time I loved somebody deeply, but I couldn't reach her. When I saw Kubrick's *2001*, I realized that I felt like those astronauts. I wrote "Space Oddity," the story of Major Tom, wandering through space alone and miserable. But not even orbiting around planet Earth did I find any traces of Z.

When Hermione left me for a dancer in February 1969, it destroyed me. I had given her so much love, and her response was to abandon me.

I COULDN'T BEAR THAT HERMIONE DIDN'T LOVE ME ANY MORE. THAT'S HOW I LEARNED WHAT HAPPENS WHEN YOU EXPOSE YOURSELF EMOTIONALLY.

Together with Mary Finnigan, a writer and journalist I occasionally went to bed with, I created an arts laboratory in Beckenham in which all kinds of creators participated. And then I flipped for an American girl I'd met: Angie Barnett. Witty, entertaining, bizarre, and uninterested in the idea of fidelity, Angie was the kind of person who didn't stop fighting until she got what she wanted. She was just what I'd been looking for. We started going out.

The promotion of *Space Oddity* brought results. The BBC retransmitted my song when a man walked on the moon. Angie insisted she'd seen Martians in the street.

In July 1969, while I was in Italy promoting the record, I received word that my father was gravely ill. I got back to London a few days before he died of pneumonia. My father, the person who had most believed in me, was gone forever.

Only three days later I had to perform at the Free Festival, an event organized by our arts laboratory. When I exited the stage and saw all those hippies counting the take, I realized I was getting tired of that scene and all those empty sermons on how to change the world.

I moved with Angie to Haddon Hall, an old mansion in Beckenham. By then I was starting to get royalties from *Space Oddity*. With the money, we surrounded ourselves with the art we both loved. Angie and I modeled our own universe in that house. There we received our lovers, and together with our friends we hatched plots and talked about ideas. Finally we decided to get married, although we agreed that it would be an open relationship in which we could see other people. I told her:

YOU KNOW I DON'T LOVE YOU, RIGHT?

But that wasn't entirely true.

Sometimes Terry would visit. Since our father's death he'd gotten worse, and my mother had confined him to an asylum, Cane Hill. My friends were surprised to learn I had a brother because I never talked about him. I was always happy when they would let him out for a family visit, but soon I realized that part of him was out there, somewhere I couldn't go. Every time he went out the door, I tortured myself asking what I could do, but I never found an answer. I composed "All the Madmen" for him.

My career had stalled again. The success of *Space Oddity* was in the past. I thought maybe Ken Pitt was too traditional in the way he promoted me, so I decided to replace him with a lawyer who promised to make me a star: Tony Defries. It hurt Ken deeply, but I didn't look back.

Newly invigorated, I shut myself up in the studio to record my third album, *The Man Who Sold the World*. I had some aces up my sleeve: guitarist Mick Ronson, whose riffs endowed my music with a new power, and producer Tony Visconti, a brilliant bassist who was becoming a good friend. But once again the record went unnoticed, and the musicians left me for other projects.

Quitting would have been the most logical response for a sensible person. Leave the dream of living from music to others. But I wasn't a sensible person. If I still wasn't good enough, I would keep working to get better. Only one person stayed at my side: Angie. I realized that she occupied more space in my heart than I wanted to admit.

In May 1971 our son was born, Duncan Zowie Haywood Jones. He was a creature full of light and life who breathed a new strength into me. As a result of that optimism, my next record was called *Hunky Dory*.

HAZY COSMIC JIVE

My new manager, Tony Defries, knew that the key to success was in America. Pitching me as the musician who would revolutionize the '70s, he got me a deal with RCA, Elvis's label. We traveled to New York to sign the papers. I went to The Factory and met Andy Warhol, who only looked at my shoes.

I dived into New York nightlife, where I met the forbidden ones portrayed in the Velvet Underground's lyrics, including Lou Reed! Although he was drunk on his arse when we met, I had a feeling that we'd go far together. To top it off, I met another musician whose daring had also affected me: Iggy Pop. Both of them had hit a career slump at that point. I started speculating about how they could fit into Defries's plans.

Back in the UK, thinking about what had happened, I felt thoroughly stimulated. Only the encounter with Warhol had been disappointing, but what did it matter that he saw nothing in me? I learned from him: he was a master of self-promotion. I had tried some stunts in the past, but it wasn't until then that I decided to really play that card. I was playing on the big stage now, so what harm was there in promoting myself with a little scandal?

So when *Melody Maker* interviewed me on January 22, 1972, I didn't hesitate to say:

I'M GAY AND I ALWAYS HAVE BEEN, INCLUDING WHEN I WAS DAVID JONES.

I knew that my declarations would attract attention, but was I lying? That night I had a dream. At the foot of my bed I observed a strange, tall being. His face was so thin that his cheekbones seemed like knives. He had red hair and a penetrating gaze, and if he harbored inner feelings, my earthling brain couldn't perceive them. He cat-hopped onto my bed with the expression tigers have, grabbed me by my wrists, and said:

I HAVE COME SO THAT YOUR PEOPLE CAN UNDERSTAND THEIR PLACE IN THE COSMOS. YOU'RE NOTHING BUT REPRESSED PRUDES. YOUR FEELINGS AND DESIRES FRIGHTEN YOU, LIKE EVERYONE OF YOUR SPECIES, BUT I'M GOING TO CHANGE THAT FOREVER. I HAVEN'T COME TO MAKE YOU GOOD PEOPLE OR PURE PEOPLE, MY LAD, I HAVE COME TO BLOW YOUR MINDS. AND YOU WILL BE MY EMISSARY.

David Bowie stopped mattering, as I became the receptacle of that beautiful bisexual alien, Ziggy Stardust.

Ziggy needed a band: the Spiders from Mars. When I told Mick Ronson, Trevor Bolder, and Woody Woodmansey that they had to wear costumes and makeup, they came up with all kinds of arguments why not. A few weeks later, they were playing together better than ever and fighting over lipstick.

The next step was to start preaching the new gospel. "Starman" was the announcement that we weren't alone in the universe. On July 6, when we played *Top of the Pops*, Ziggy reached out his arm and put it affectionately around Mick's shoulders. Many in the TV audience were scandalized; others saw it as a messianic act: the new era had arrived.

The following weeks were frantic. I got on stage and turned Ziggy loose. No doubts, nothing to worry about: the extraterrestrial was performing, not me. By concert's end, the audience members had become messengers of our cause.

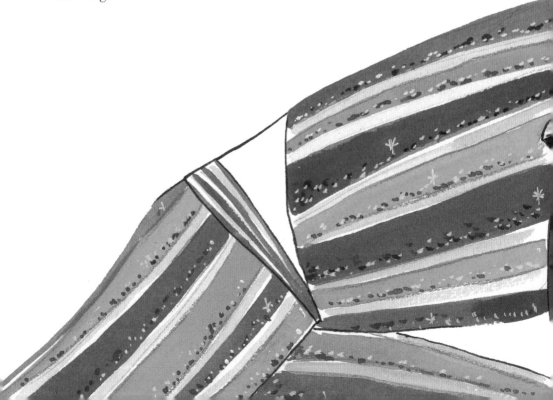

The tour was a smash. England surrendered to the alien. The next step was to assault the most powerful nation on Earth. Tony Defries was convinced that to become a star I had to present myself like one, and he prepared the North American tour in high style. We crossed the ocean on a transatlantic liner, stayed in the best hotels, rented luxurious limousines.

As the fatigue and stress of the tour set in, things got weird. Angie was angry about the fans who were all over me after every concert, but what did she expect? We had an open relationship, and I was a rock star. She started picking her lovers out of my entourage to provoke my jealousy, and we argued hatefully.

Every day there was a new problem. Spiders Trevor and Woodmansey mutinied when they found out they were getting paid less than the musicians who had joined us in America. Defries managed to placate them with promises of a raise, but I saw how easily the band could sabotage the tour.

We went back to London for Christmas, and I used the time to try to put my marriage back together; I wanted to make things better, although I was getting tired of Angie's tantrums. My next record, *Aladdin Sane*, reflected the split personality I had acquired as a result of harboring Ziggy and, although I never realized it, my darkest thoughts about Terry's schizophrenia.

THE ALBUM TITLE'S PUN WAS ATTUNED TO MY SPLIT PERSONALITY: *ALADDIN SANE* IS INDISTINGUISHABLE FROM *A LAD INSANE.*

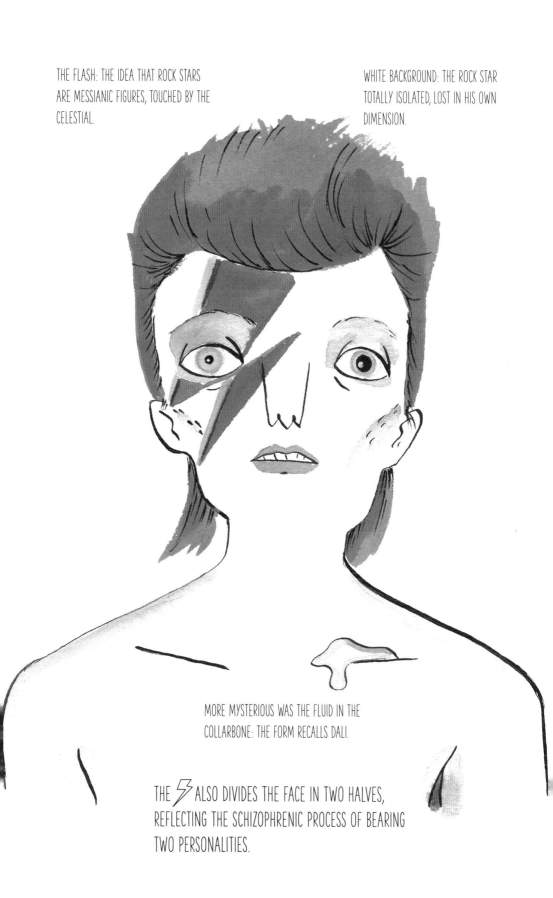

THE FLASH: THE IDEA THAT ROCK STARS ARE MESSIANIC FIGURES, TOUCHED BY THE CELESTIAL.

WHITE BACKGROUND: THE ROCK STAR TOTALLY ISOLATED, LOST IN HIS OWN DIMENSION.

MORE MYSTERIOUS WAS THE FLUID IN THE COLLARBONE: THE FORM RECALLS DALI.

THE ⚡ ALSO DIVIDES THE FACE IN TWO HALVES, REFLECTING THE SCHIZOPHRENIC PROCESS OF BEARING TWO PERSONALITIES.

When I resumed the tour, I decided it was best to have Angie remain in Europe. There were more attempted uprisings by Woody and Trevor, but Mick Ronson interceded so that Defries would fulfill his promises of a raise as well as promise Mick a solo album. I had a bad feeling about all this.

The tour went on and on. We went to Japan, and from there we went west to Berlin, where you could still see the damage from the bombardments thirty years before. The city's visible wounds connected with my interior state.

On returning to North America, we learned that RCA had suspended the 1973 tour. Apparently we spent too much money. I knew nothing about it because Defries was in charge of the accounting, but that had obviously been an error on my part. On top of that, Angie was furious with me after she made a surprise trip to New York and found me in bed with my new lover, Ava Cherry.

I WANTED IT ALL TO STOP. I ASPIRED TO A VERY DIFFERENT KIND OF PROJECT. I WAS EXHAUSTED, AND ABSOLUTELY BORED WITH THE CONCEPT OF ZIGGY.

When we got back to the UK I had made a drastic decision. If my bassist and my drummer thought they could screw me, I'd get out in front of them. On July 3, 1973, in a concert at the Hammersmith Odeon, I announced:

NOT ONLY IS THIS THE LAST SHOW OF THE TOUR, IT'S THE LAST SHOW THAT WE'LL EVER DO. THANK YOU.

The Spiders ceased to exist. The only one who'd been told was Ronson.

Back in the dressing room, I looked in the mirror. Ziggy was there before me: exhausted and faded. After months of contamination on Earth, the alien was dying. I smiled contemptuously when I saw his lost gaze, which seemed a cry for help. He was lacking air like a clownfish that had escaped the aquarium. My right hand crossed into the mirror and grabbed his swan neck. My fingers tensed around his throat. The creature had no strength to resist.

"You're not a revelation any more," I told him. "You're bloated. You're an ego written in glitter."

Ziggy's body fell lifeless to the floor. I lit a cigarette, and for a moment I was at peace.

THE SIDE EFFECTS OF THE COCAINE

The record company didn't care about my boredom. I was contractually obligated to deliver an album, so I decided to do one of '60s covers: *Pin Ups*. We recorded in a lovely castle in France, which allowed me to get away from Angie's eternal jealousy for a while. As we were finishing up the project, I realized that playing rock star was less and less fun. Even Mick Ronson's powerful guitar seemed repetitive. I needed new experiences, musical and otherwise.

In 1974, Angie, Zowie, and I moved to Chelsea. When I wasn't making media appearances, I was reading George Orwell. Bit by bit, a vision came into my mind.

I SAW THE CITIES OF ENGLAND TRASHED AND DESTROYED. FILTH AND SILENCE HAD TAKEN OVER THE RUINS OF THE OPULENT TWENTIETH CENTURY. ANCIENT VEHICLES LAY ABANDONED, RUSTED, WITHOUT A DROP OF PETROL IN THEIR TANKS. WITHIN THAT SKELETON OF BRICK, CONCRETE, AND STEEL, HUMANS WERE TURNING INTO MONSTERS FROM RADIATION. THOSE WHO HADN'T SUCCUMBED TO MADNESS LIVED IN THE LAST CORNERS, SWELTERING AND FULL OF FLEAS.

My style was getting more experimental at the same time that it was getting closer to the black music that had fascinated me in my younger days.

And I had started consuming a substance that was omnipresent in my world: cocaine. It made my mind work faster and gave me energy during the interminable sessions for *Diamond Dogs*. It was stupendous.

Just before the album came out, I moved back to New York. I took up with Ava Cherry again and started connecting with the soul and R&B scene. I met Carlos Alomar, a brilliant Puerto Rican guitarist who, when he saw the bags under my eyes and my emaciated physique, invited me to his house so his wife could feed me.

My style kept transforming. With each new concert, my sound got closer to soul and funk.

I WAS NOT
DISGUISED
AS A GOUSTER,
I WAS BECOMING
ONE.

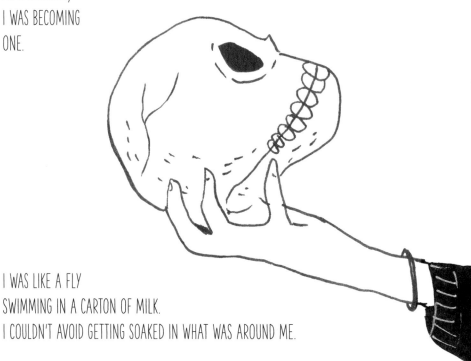

I WAS LIKE A FLY
SWIMMING IN A CARTON OF MILK.
I COULDN'T AVOID GETTING SOAKED IN WHAT WAS AROUND ME.

The shows could be exhausting, but cocaine fixed that. Plus, I had a new ally: my personal assistant Corinne Schwab, Coco, who occupied herself with my career with a ferocity and loyalty that no one up till then had ever displayed. She knew how to protect me.

With Ava Cherry, Carlos Alomar, Mike Garson, and other musicians I realized my dream of making an album of black music: *Young Americans*. The album sold wonderfully, and I became the first white artist to play on *Soul Train*. Being in the spotlight made it possible for me to collaborate with all kinds of artists, even Cher. Who would have thought that little David Jones, with his ears always glued to the record player, would one day be here? Finally all my work and dedication were bearing fruit. I was excited.

At times I tried to slip away from Ava to meet other girls, but jealousy always followed me. Angie came to visit me in Philadelphia, and when she saw Ava there she became furious. We had a serious fight. She screamed and screamed at me, while I withstood the deluge by laying out a pair of white lines. When she saw that her verbal abuse had no effect, she threatened to kill herself. I was sick of her endless cries for attention.

For months I hadn't been able to reconcile the money that was coming in from MainMan, Defries's company, so I had a sitdown meeting with him to find out what was happening. That's when I realized how much of a disaster the contract was that I signed in 1972. Rather than just representing me, Tony had created a company in which I was no more than a mere employee. This bloodsucker had been getting rich, and I only got the crumbs. But he had me tied up. To get out of it, there was no alternative to giving him all my masters to date and a percentage of my future records until 1982. David Bowie wound up being a slave for a company built on his own talent.

I remember passing the subsequent weeks in Ava's arms or next to Coco. Whatever they said to console me, if I listened, I've forgotten it. I only know that while they were talking, I dragged myself over to the nearest paper packet and sniffed that miraculous powder in the hope that I'd stop feeling like shit. Then everything got blurry.

I moved to Los Angeles. The demons followed me there, but I protected myself by following a strict diet of milk and peppers, and reading a lot. With the blinds closed tight so as not to let in the depressing California sun, I drew protective signs, and if a dark spirit came in, I did an exorcism. Angie came to collaborate in the rituals.

For months the darkness was right next to me. I heard people I couldn't see; I discovered witches among my admirers who wanted my semen for their sabbath; a shadow spoke in the voice of my brother, Terry, warning me that I was headed for a place where there were only screams and hopelessness. When I could take no more, I snorted coke to be able to keep resisting. But the suffering continued, one day and another and another. Finally, I closed my eyes and let the nightmares invade me. I was afraid of being in that dark place forever, so I begged the Light to protect me.

THESE WERE THE DARKEST DAYS OF MY LIFE. I WAS SUBMERGED IN MISERY. REMEMBERING IT IS TOO PAINFUL.

But when I would wake up, I still had my awareness, which had not drowned in the madness. I continued being David Bowie. In those moments of lucidity I was conscious of the disaster that cocaine was conjuring in my life.

Even in the depths of that snake pit, my hunger to create kept me from sinking forever. I had passed a good part of 1975 and 1976 living a nightmare, but I also had some great accomplishments. My first movie, *The Man Who Fell to Earth*, received very good reviews. In it I became Thomas Jerome Newton, who had come to our planet in order to save his own and who was, like me, incapable of feeling. I recorded *Station to Station* and made new friends, like John Lennon. He was the key to writing "Fame," and it was precisely in matters of fame that he became a great ally. I think John saw in me a younger version of himself, and for me it was great to have a new older brother.

But it was with another friend, Jim Osterberg, the person behind the savage Iggy Pop, that I decided to escape. I had visited him from time to time in the psychiatric hospital where he was detoxing, and when he got out, he'd been put in jail for stealing food. He was as deep into the powder as I was.

"How about we get out of here?" I asked him.

"Where are we gonna go?" he asked me.

I remembered the image of that cold city, scarred by its desolate history.

BERLIN, WE'LL GO TO BERLIN.

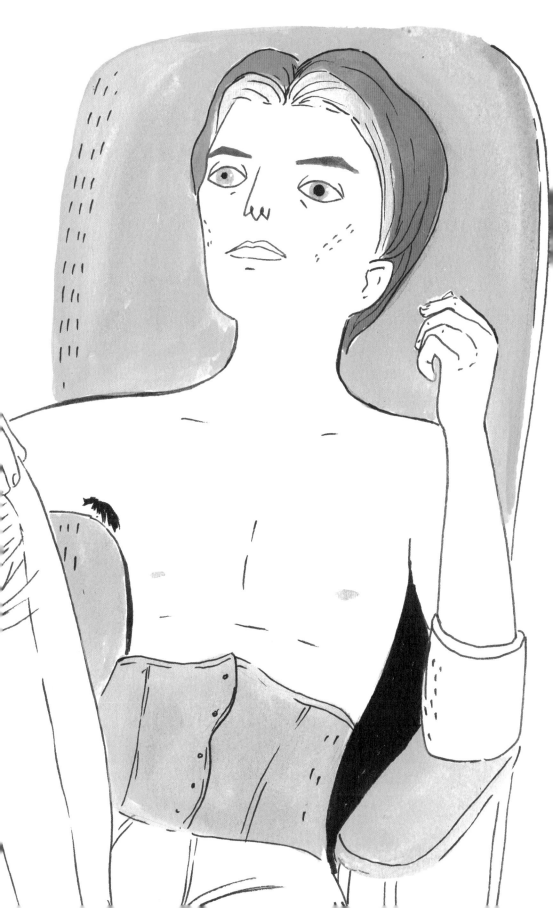

STANDING BY THE WALL

At last the time had come to close the occult philosophy books and return to the world of the living. The *Station to Station* tour took me back to Europe.

Jim and I went on a train trip across the continent to Moscow. The landscapes and people passing by outside the window engraved themselves into my brain: they seemed anchored in the past. The KGB followed our footsteps. Everything was cold and distant.

The skies and cities of Eastern Europe were aligned with the state of my soul. The love that I gave or received never soothed my internal emptiness. I decided to let it be: I had to learn to live with myself.

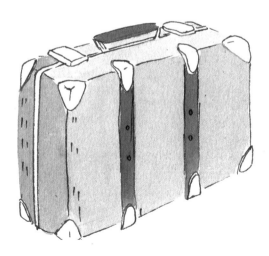

When I returned to London, I saw with a certain satisfaction that a flock of fans had come to Victoria Station to receive me. I saluted them from a convertible.

SOME IDIOT USED THE PHOTO OF ME WITH MY HAND UPRAISED, AND THE CAPTION READ: "IS BOWIE A NAZI?"

It was incredible: I was coming back from the United States after two years of paying homage to soul, funk, and R&B, a long romance with Ava Cherry, and immersion in African American culture, and now they called me a Nazi.

Yes, I had made declarations calling for a strong leader for England; I shared the idea that Hitler had been the first rock star, and I continued to be fascinated by Nazi symbology, but besides forming part of my cocaine psychosis, all that was nothing but infrastructure for my creation. In my songs it was clear that I wasn't yearning for the return of fascism. I was going to have to learn to be more careful about how I represented myself.

Angie had painstakingly searched for a lovely place for us to live in Blonay, Switzerland. As soon as I crossed the threshold I realized I didn't want to live there. So Iggy and I moved to Château d'Hérouville, where I had recorded *Pin Ups* three years earlier. Only Coco and essential staff came along. Zowie spent some time with us.

Iggy and I were getting high less. We concentrated our energies on what would be his first solo record, *The Idiot*, for which I assumed production responsibilities.

As we finished it, the sound I wanted for my next record was becoming clear in my mind. A couple of years previously I had discovered Kraftwerk, a German group that created a sound that was at once dehumanized and suggestive. It was just what I wanted. I got the necessary musicians together, among them Carlos Alomar and Tony Visconti, but the key was Brian Eno. The former Roxy Music member, my competition in the Ziggy era, had embarked on an experimental path that led him to create a minimalist music he called *ambient*.

BRIAN APPLIED TO HIS WORK EVERYTHING THAT HE'D LEARNED IN ART SCHOOL, AND I THOUGHT: "LET'S SEE IF WE CAN ALSO DESTROY THAT PART OF THE CULTURE."

When we applied the musicians' skill to Eno's new-music ideas, hallucinatory sounds appeared.

I knew the record company wasn't going to like my new work, but I didn't care. The time of fame and promotion had ended. I wanted to make my music, and *Low* was the declaration of my intentions.

NOW I FELT FREER. I HAD ONLY NEEDED TO MAKE A POSITIVE DECISION TO THROW MYSELF INTO DOING WHAT I WANTED TO DO AND NOT WHAT WAS EXPECTED OF BOWIE OR ANY OF HIS PERSONAS.

In those songs I was howling from the open wounds in Los Angeles and what I'd seen behind the Iron Curtain. As a response to what we were conjuring, the castle where we were recording reacted by unleashing all kinds of supernatural phenomena. With so many ghosts hanging out, I failed to notice that my son, Zowie, was growing up without any stable platform. I only realized it when Carlos Alomar was leaving the castle after recording; Zowie asked him if he was going to forget him. I felt terribly sad, and from then on I tried to be more involved in his life.

Tony Visconti and I went to Studio Hansa to finish the new record. At last we were in Berlin. Neither Jim nor I spent much time studying the hit parade. Berlin called, and we moved through it like alley cats. We spent hours in its cafes and cabarets.

We had an exceptional guide, Romy Haag, who soon fell into my web of seduction. She seemed airlifted out of 1930s Berlin. We took in everything the city could offer. We went on sprees, but never completely lost control. I watched so that the dope pushers of Berlin didn't get next to Jim, and he did the same with me. That's how things were: each one looking out for the other.

IGGY AND I HAD SERIOUS PROBLEMS WITH DRUGS. TO GET CLEAN WE WENT TO BERLIN, WORLD CAPITAL OF HEROIN.

Jim walked eight miles a day to stay in shape. I liked to get lost in the foreign workers' neighborhoods and spend hours in their cramped shops without anyone recognizing me. Then we would rendezvous and catch each other up on our day.

The immigrants, the cabarets, and a concrete wall that divided the city in half: all that was Berlin. I couldn't stop imagining a pair of lovers defying that structure of barbed wire and mistrust by kissing in front of the wall. That idea grew into "Heroes," an anthem proclaiming that nothing is more transgressive than love between two people.

Despite the promo campaign about how there was New Wave, there was Old Wave, and then there was Bowie, RCA didn't make much money on *"Heroes."* But I was satisfied with this most productive phase. In a year I had recorded four albums that would go down in history: *The Idiot, Low, Lust for Life*, and *"Heroes."* I was full of the music I was making, and I had the delicious consolation of knowing that Defries was making less and less money from my work.

Things were changing. Drugs were no longer a threat to my physical survival or mental stability. I had the sensation of having laid down

crushing burdens and, as if everything was falling into place, my relationship with Angie at last ended.

In an interview she accused me of having struck Zowie during the Christmas holidays in 1977. Shaming me in the tabloids like that was a declaration of war. The rage I felt during those days dissolved the last memories I had of the tenderness and love that Angie and I had shared over the years. All our attempts to put it back together had failed. I decided to do what I'd always done: turn the page.

PUT A BULLET IN MY BRAIN AND
IT MAKES ALL THE PAPERS

Little by little, Angie's shadow faded. Zowie and I began a new life. We both needed a rest, and I wanted my son's eyes to light up with luminous discoveries. The African landscapes and wild fauna that appeared in his books could be a good way to start, so we went to spend some time in Kenya.

Musically, I continued experimenting with Eno, and the album *Lodger* wasn't bad. But I kept feeling that itch, and by now I knew what it was: the constant necessity of changing my plumage. Maybe a tour would let me come up with some new ideas, and I could use it to record a live album and work off my commitment to RCA. I wanted off the label. I had enough prestige to get the musicians I wanted, like Adrian Belew, a guitarist I'd met at a Frank Zappa concert. Zappa was not pleased. I felt like a chess player moving pieces slowly and carefully to regain control of my life.

That meant distancing myself from many friends and musical idols who were drifting because of drugs. One was Iggy and another was Lou Reed. When Lou asked me to produce the album he was writing, like I had done years before with *Transformer*, I told him it depended on whether he was willing to stop doing drugs. He got up, furious, and slapped me. How dare I talk to him like that? he shouted. Before I could smack him back, he was out of the bar. But I wasn't going to leave it there. I went to the hotel where he was staying and waited for him to come out of his room and we'd finish the fight. Since he was too much of a coward to face me, I paid him back by stealing a guitarist from him too.

The '70s were over and I was relieved to have survived them, though not without damage. What would the future bring? Some people in my situation would have read their tea leaves or cloaked themselves in nostalgia. I went to work.

I moved back to New York. I spent more and more time with Lennon and Yoko. We'd had similar experiences, and we understood each other perfectly. The baby-brother affection I had for John grew. It was good not to feel alone.

And my career was moving. My next album, *Scary Monsters*, was a big hit. The critics loved it, and it sold.

As a declaration of intentions, in the single "Ashes to Ashes" I buried all the heroes I'd created in the '60s.

Living off my past was not an option.

Hoping to develop my acting, I accepted an important theatrical role. My next disguise was that of Joseph Merrick, the "Elephant Man," and the stage was on Broadway. Merrick had a fascinating backstory; it was when I saw his skull on display at the University of London that I knew how to approach the role. The other cast members expected to find themselves in rehearsals with a rock star who had been cast for publicity reasons, but it didn't take long to convince them that beneath the Bowie label was a complete artist who had been hard at work for years and years.

The reviews were excellent, and the same actors who had been wary of me now treated me like one of the club. During one performance, when I had to get into the bathtub I saw they had slipped porn mags and a vibrator in it just to watch me try to repress my laughter.

Then an unexpected blow changed everything forever. Watching the news, I tried to convince myself it was a joke: John Lennon, the greatest person on the face of the Earth, was shot by a moron. I had lost a source of inspiration, someone who had been there for me in difficult moments, and one of my few authentic friends. How could the world kill someone whose art had filled it with such life? There were rumors: Mark Chapman, the assassin, had attended a performance of *The Elephant Man*, and my name appeared on his list. Suddenly I only wanted one thing: to seclude myself whenever I could.

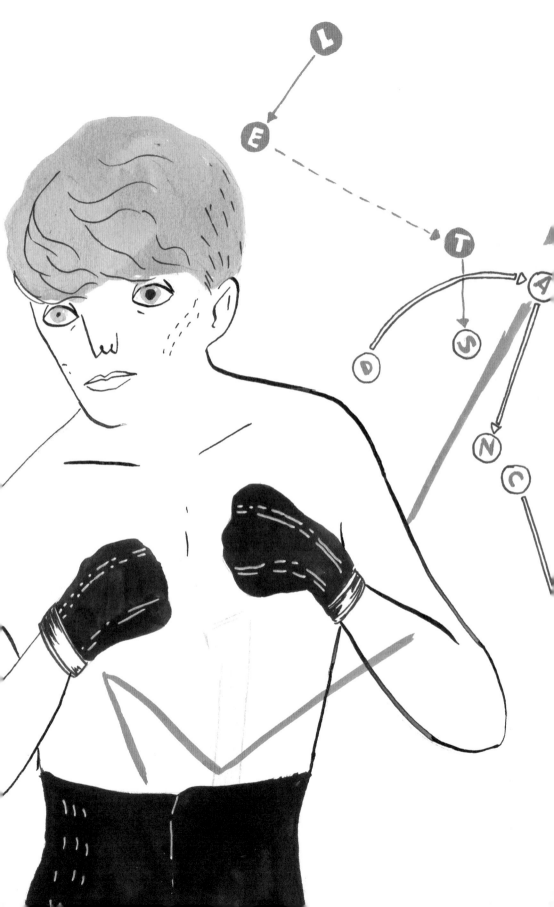

DANCING WITH THE BIG BOYS

I lay low for a while. There was nothing I wanted to show to an audience. I just wanted to rest and think. The ideal place to do that was Switzerland, and the ideal company was my son. By now he didn't want

to be called Zowie, but Joey. He was reaching adolescence; to become an adult he had to get rid of the burden of being the son of Bowie. It was stupendous watching him develop his own personality.

In Switzerland I reconnected with some more of my pupils: Queen. Freddie Mercury and I had met in the late '60s at a flea market when we were nobodies. Things had changed plenty for everyone.

We started improvising in the studio and came up with "Under Pressure." We knew it would be a hit, but I gave them the rights. It wasn't an altruistic decision: I just didn't want MainMan to make the money.

My extended rest period allowed me to reconnect with two people I had been far away from: my mother and Terry. She was happy to see me again; since my father died we hadn't spent much time together. With my brother things were harder: he'd attempted suicide, throwing himself from a window at Cane Hill. When I went to visit him, he seemed pleased, but it was hard for me to look into his prematurely aged eyes. They seemed like hostages of his terrible illness, imploring me for some kind of aid I couldn't supply.

I DON'T KNOW HOW MUCH OF IT IS MADNESS. I BELIEVE THAT THERE'S A TERRIBLE STORE OF EMOTIONAL AND SPIRITUAL MUTILATION IN MY FAMILY THAT HAS TAKEN HOLD OF ME IN DIFFERENT WAYS OVER THE YEARS.

But there was still the hope and consolation of being able to help my son. After he spent some days being ignored by Angie and her then lover during a visit in 1984, he decided not to see her any more. Coping with the lack of maternal love was something he would have to overcome on his own, but I, for my part, was not going to fail him.

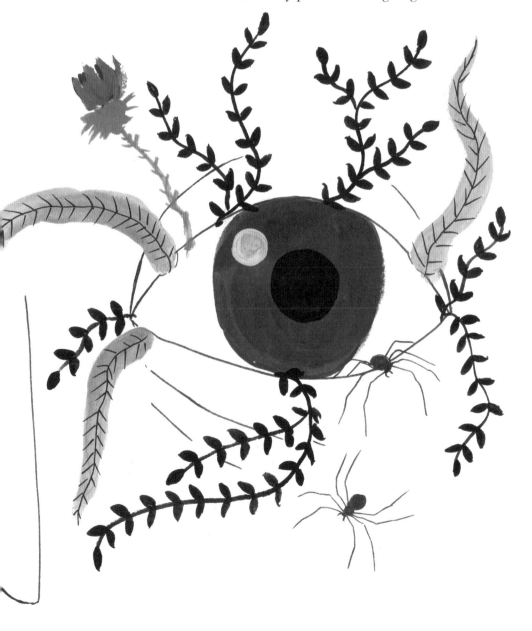

At last the moment arrived to take complete charge of my career. When my debt with MainMan had been liquidated and my contract with RCA rescinded, I got ready to make up for lost time and money. Freddie Mercury had promised to be a go-between for me and his label, EMI, and I needed a record to seduce them with. I knew who I wanted at my side. Nile Rodgers had blown up playing funky music with his band Chic and then distinguished himself as a producer. I made it clear to Nile that I wanted to make hits. And we did. EMI was thrilled with the album *Let's Dance*, and I received $17 million as an advance! The tour we embarked on, *Serious Moonlight*, was impressive: sixteen countries, ninety-six concerts, two and half million tickets. We filled stadiums night after night. Most of those fans had just discovered me through songs like "Let's Dance" or "Modern Love," which came accompanied with video clips that I had supervised down to the last detail. Few of them had heard of Brian Eno or Kraftwerk. Of course there were those who accused me of having gone commercial, as if my only function in life were to create the music they needed. But I was as happy as a kid to be on the front lines of pop.

My next album was *Tonight*. While I was out promoting it, I received the painful news that Terry had killed himself. He escaped from Cane Hill and lay down on the train tracks to end his suffering. I had just turned thirty-eight.

I decided not to go to his funeral. I didn't want to turn my brother's death into a show and be forced into the role of suffering superstar. I sent a crown that said,

YOU'VE SEEN MORE THINGS THAN WE CAN IMAGINE, BUT ALL THESE MOMENTS WILL BE LOST, LIKE TEARS WASHED AWAY BY THE RAIN. GOD BLESS YOU.

The press crucified me: I was a cold being who had turned his back on his family and abandoned his brother for years. Who were they to know what I felt? Where were they when Terry began to suffer? Did they have any idea how frustrated I was each time I saw him and realized that I was losing him little by little?

That wasn't enough for them. Airing out David Bowie's dirty laundry had become a lucrative activity. After Terry died they started digging, and all my family's mental problems came to light. That was terribly painful, even more so when I found out that people I cherished, like Tony Visconti or Lindsay Kemp, had cooperated with the authors of those books. I felt betrayed. Anybody in my vicinity could play the game of making me into an amusement park attraction.

That was the price of being a global pop star.

But I wasn't going to disappear down a hole. In 1985 I participated in the solidarity concert Live Aid in Wembley Stadium. I gave up part of my performance time to show a video about famine in Ethiopia, and the donations picked up. I dedicated "Heroes" to Joey and all the children of the world.

That same year I acted in the movie *Labyrinth*. Since so many people thought I was a heartless monster, I decided to become one, and I delighted in being the villain in a children's story.

I also appeared in *Absolute Beginners*, set in the 1950s, in which I played a ruthless publicist.

In 1987 I went back into the studio and recorded *Never Let Me Down*. The result bored me so much that I thought about quitting and dedicating myself to my other great passion, painting. Escaping into my work, though, I kept touring and prepared what the times called for, the most dazzling spectacle possible: the Glass Spider tour. It featured an enormous spider of glass fiber, blinding lights, and dancers descending the threads. The money it made was only comparable with the colossal boredom the musicians and I felt.

I LOVED THE MONEY I WAS MAKING AND IT WAS OBVIOUS THAT TO KEEP ON MAKING IT I WOULD HAVE TO GIVE PEOPLE WHAT THEY WANTED. BUT I WAS DRYING UP AS AN ARTIST.

In October of that year came one of the bitterest episodes of my life as a star. Wanda Lee Nichols, a girl who had come on the tour with us and with whom I had gone to bed, accused me of rape. The jury rejected her accusation, but it outlined another lesson: I was a profitable star and was vulnerable to this kind of accusation. My nights of continual conquest had to stop.

Once that odious tour was over, we burned the enormous spider and felt liberated. The show was over, and the musicians went home to their families.

Me, I'd reached the goal I laid down for myself in 1983: I would never have to worry about money again. But the price was that I'd lost interest in creating. And although for a while I was with Melissa Hurley, nineteen years younger than I, something didn't fit. Deep down, I continued feeling alone.

A HEART FOR THE TIN MAN

I had lost contact with my creative instinct. The only solution was to become monkish about my work habits and start all over. The opportunity came to me via Reeves Gabrels, a guitarist with a simple style whom I'd met through his wife, a publicist who worked with me on *Glass Spider*. I suggested we work together, and a new project took shape in my mind. We brought in the brothers Tony and Hunt Sales, who had worked with Iggy and me on *Lust for Life*. That was the beginning of Tin Machine. Our intention was to play live.

EMI was displeased by that move, but I wasn't going to be intimidated, and we released our LP in 1989. We recorded it in the Bahamas and premiered it in a little bar in Nassau, where we played for fifty or so astonished tourists. We decided the tour should be intimate, and we'd develop it in clubs and small spots in different countries.

The critics were perplexed, but I was truly enjoying making music. I needed to stop being Bowie the brand and be part of something that didn't orbit around me.

With the new decade around the corner and the other members of Tin Machine resting up, I had the idea of a solo retrospective tour. Once the tour ended, I went to yet another of those parties that were everywhere in those days, and I met a woman who would change my life forever: Iman Mohamed Abdulmajid.

As far as I was concerned, there was nothing else going on at that party but our conversation. How many disguises had I put on in my life, one on top of the other? Iman took them all down. The superstar, the millionaire, the irresistible seducer, she struck them away with a glance. She had seen so much, from the misery of Africa to the glamor of the runway. She wasn't afraid of David Bowie.

Iman didn't stop until she had seen completely through me. When I had no more masks, I showed her what was hiding beneath: the alien, isolated on a planet where he had never fit; that was the real me. But she hadn't finished with me. She unzipped a zipper that I had forgotten existed, and the gray skin of the extraterrestrial fell to the floor.

Beneath it was David Robert Jones. She smiled, satisfied.

We moved in together quickly. My life as a musician kept moving forward: a new tour with Tin Machine, conflicts with the record company, bandmates who abused drugs.

But none of that was my priority now. My principal objective was to ask for the hand of the person with whom I wanted to spend the rest of my life.

Iman and I married in April 1992. "Now we are us. And after that, everyone else," I told her. It was a private civil ceremony in Switzerland, and in June we celebrated our union in Florence with the people who mattered most to us: my mother, my son (by now called Duncan, in time he became the godson of my new wife), Iman's family, and all our friends. The magazine *Hello!* ran a twenty-three-page spread about the wedding.

Iman was radiant. I had never seen her so luminous.

We decided to look for a house in Los Angeles. But the city was in chaos after the riots over the police beating of Rodney King. I saw it as the worst side of the United States: police beating a young black man. Iman and I decided to set ourselves up in New York.

Iman brought me sufficient tranquility to make peace with my own life. While I was recording my next album, *Black Tie White Noise*, I felt again that tug toward experimentation, and almost without realizing it, for the first time I could get close to the things that caused me pain: years after his death, I let out my feelings of failure and blame about Terry in the song "Jump They Say."

I HAD FOUND LIBERTY IN MY LIFE ACCEPTING IT THE WAY IT WAS, NOT GOING ON A QUEST FOR A HOLY GRAIL THAT WOULD PROVIDE SOME TRUTH THAT, I THOUGHT, I NEEDED MORE THAN OTHER TRUTHS.

I met up again with people from my past. Those were the dark years of AIDS; since the early '80s we had all lost many friends. In the tribute concert to Freddie Mercury at Wembley I sang "Heroes" with Queen and Mick Ronson, my old guitarist, and at the end of the song I knelt before that immense public to say a paternoster for the afflicted.

I found the courage to take my work to the places I wanted to. Brian Eno and I visited Guggin, a mental hospital in Austria that had an interesting therapeutic program in collaboration with minority artists. If only Terry could have had something like that at Cane Hill. Would it have helped him to exorcise his demons? How much of my art had been nothing more than an attempt to understand my brother's illness? However it was, ideas were always buzzing in my head, and they ended up in my work, over and over.

In the next album, *1.Outside*, which I released in 1995, I tried to reflect the confusion of century's end, a confusion I enjoyed; I had always mistrusted closed-off discourse.

That same year in London I presented my first individual gallery show as a painter. My incursion into the art world was taken as an affront by some connoisseurs, who saw me as a poser and accused me of trading on my notoriety. But I had sufficient resources with which to retaliate. Three years later I was part of a campaign to reevaluate the work of Nat Tate, an obscure midcentury painter. Some critics confirmed the value of the unknown artist only to learn hours later that Nat Tate had never existed; he was an invention we, four art lovers, created to show what a bunch of posers these supposedly erudite ones were. I could only smile at the ridiculousness. Not in vain had I managed concepts of disguise and simulation over the decades, and I knew how to flush out the real fakes.

WORLD WIDE BOWIE

I had dozens of critics, but my admirers were legion. At century's end, I was happily married and had a solid career behind me.

Groups that appeared in those years, like Suede and Placebo, considered me one of their main influences. My career was still important to me, but my family was even more important. The more time I spent with Iman, the more we loved each other, and the calmer and happier I felt. The only addiction I held onto was tobacco; I smoked two packs a day, and I knew that if I didn't quit there would be consequences for my voice and my health.

I was getting older, but I was full of energy. I was also capable of seeing the events of previous years with a new perspective. In summer 1996 I made peace with Lou Reed: there was no point in being enemies because of a fight fifteen years earlier over those damned drugs, so I could count on him for my fiftieth birthday party. I gave a concert in Madison Square Garden, with, besides the "king of New York," several of the musicians I had influenced: Dave Grohl, Billy Corgan, Frank Black. Robert Smith, the leader of the Cure, gave me a curious present: a fossilized chameleon. But the present that most moved me came from Iman: she had discreetly contacted my old friends, and they put together a book filled with dedications and drawings.

Iman and I wanted children. Sooner or later she'd get pregnant, so it was time to focus on my estate. The rights to my records before 1976, as well as the masters, were still in the hands of Tony Defries. I knew my ex-manager wasn't going to let them go cheap, so I had to get some money. Lots of money. A high figure, even for me. I hit on an idea that no musician had tried before: to make my catalog an object of invest-ment—Bowie bonds. Basically, I assigned my income from songwriting for ten years to whoever wanted the pleasure. An investment group put in $55 million.

> I CREATE ART AND THEN I SELL IT.
> WHEN I'M CREATING,
> I'M 100 PERCENT ARTIST
> AND WHEN I'M SELLING,
> I'M 100 PERCENT IMPRESARIO.

I invested part of the money and with the rest—more than $20 million—I paid Defries to get my work back.

Tony Defries had definitively exited my life, and all my albums belonged to me at last. I had the comfort of knowing they would be part of my children's inheritance.

As the new millennium approached, money from my work kept pouring in. Shortly after my birthday in 1997 I released *Earthling*. I kept participating in movies and all kinds of TV shows.

And there were new tools to experiment with. I spent hours and hours on the internet. Its possibilities were inexhaustible, even for me. Part of me wished I had been born in the '90s in order to have become an artist on the net. While most of my peers from my generation didn't understand computers, I pioneered a virtual community, gathering my followers together in bowienet. My page allowed me to talk with them from the security of my home and discover potential collaborators.

Computers were opening up a whole new world of expressive possibilities. When I got a proposal to create a soundtrack for the videogame *Omikron*, I was delighted. Iman, Reeves Gabrels, and I became characters in the game! Later, Reeves and I decided to create a new record out of this soundtrack: *"hours . . ."*

But something else happened that year, not related to my career or technology. After many disappointments and all kinds of artificial techniques, Iman got pregnant naturally at the end of 1999. Nothing could have made us happier.

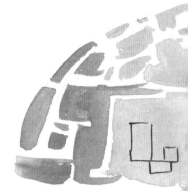

NEVER GET OLD

In August 2000 our daughter, Alexandria, was born. She had her mother's beauty. Many fans expressed the desire to share our happiness by sending gifts for her. I urged them to donate the gifts to Save the Children instead. The moment I saw her, I vowed: I'd be the father she needed. I wouldn't repeat the mistakes I had made with Duncan. I kept on working and creating, but Iman and Lexi would be my priority.

WHEN YOU'RE YOUNG YOU WORRY ABOUT MANY THINGS, INCLUDING YOURSELF. AS YOU GET OLDER YOU START THINKING OF FEWER THINGS AS IMPORTANT, BESIDES THE FUNDAMENTALS. ONE OF THOSE IS TO LOVE THE PEOPLE WHO MATTER TO YOU, TO WORRY ABOUT THE SURVIVAL OF YOUR CLOSEST FAMILY. AFTER THEM, YOUR FRIENDS AND THEN THE OUTER CIRCLES, LIKE WAVES ON WATER.

My mother died eight months after Alexandria was born, at the age of eighty-eight. My relationship with her had always been worse than with Terry or Dad, but we had long since reconciled. She lived a long life. Unlike my father, she got to see her grandchildren. I said goodbye to her peacefully.

Now there was no one left from my old family. Now we were only Duncan, Alexandria, Iman, and me.

Being a full-time father had another effect on me: I started to worry about the world in a way I never had before. What would my daughter find when she grew up? What would she think of my generation when she was older? It had been years since I composed quickly. My reflections about the reality waiting for Lexi never arrived at a conclusion, but they became the substrate of my lyrics. There was plenty of material. Visconti and I went to a newly opened studio in Shokan, New York, two hours from the city, close enough that I could get back home fast if I needed to. There, surrounded by nature—one morning, I woke up early and saw through the window a pair of deer grazing!—the songs came along at a good clip.

But the recording of *Heathen* was interrupted by the horrible news we saw over and over on TV: the attack on the Twin Towers. The first thing I did was call Iman. She was fine, although terrified. Between sobs and shouts, she told me she had just seen the second plane slam into the World Trade Center. Then the call was cut off. It took Visconti almost a day to be able to talk with his family. From our studio we could see the smoke rising from our city. One of the bloodiest terrorist attacks in history had happened a few blocks from our home.

When Tony and I got back to New York, I saw the steel and concrete remains of the World Trade Center. A memory came back to me: the ruins of London where I played as a child.

It was an honor to open the Concert for New York in Madison Square Garden in October. "Heroes" sounded very different that day. We were thinking of those who died in the city I thought of as mine, like the firemen at the corner of our house who always waved to Lexi and now would never come back.

After the release of *Heathen,* I went on tour again. Soon after, I was already at work composing *Reality.* Not a year had passed since the end of the tour, and I was already elated with the idea of going back out. I exercised and meditated. I even stopped smoking, with Iman's help. The great world tour began in October 2003.

But something started going wrong. In some concerts I had the sensation of seeing a shadow in the corner of my eye, a darkness in the wings of the stage. By year's end I had to cancel five concerts because of the flu.

Not only did the shadow in the corner not disappear, it got more frequent and denser. And the stumbles continued. In June, in Oslo, I almost stopped a concert when some idiot in the audience threw a lollipop that hit me in the left eye. Five days later, in Prague, I couldn't stop seeing that black cloud. It no longer hid in my peripheral vision but now obscured everything. At the beginning of the concert I felt a horrible pain in my chest that kept building. Despite my decades of professionalism, I had no strength to keep singing, and I had to leave the stage.

The doctors told me I had suffered a pinched nerve in the shoulder. It could be a symptom of cardiological complications. Behind the doctors, I saw the shadow, whirling.

I decided to continue the tour, but I was very worried.

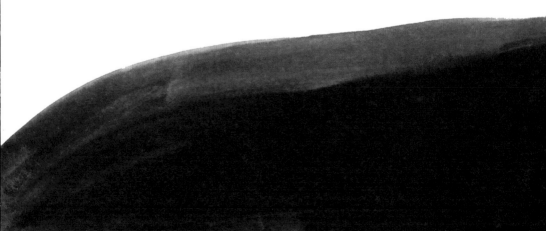

Two days later, in Scheessel, Germany, I went on stage in pain. The songs didn't sound as strong as usual. I tried to forget the pain and focus on singing, but the shadow wouldn't let me. It covered the stage, the audience, like a sea of black fog, and finally it blocked out the sky. There was only the shadow, a damp silence, and me.

I understood that the darkness had always been there. Not only since the beginning of the tour, but always. It had waited, crouching in the corner, for its moment. And now it was letting me know.

But then it went away. It had only been a warning.

Light and sound returned to the stage, and I was in Scheessel again, although I saw through a dark filter. My chest was bothering me a lot. When the concert ended I left the stage and collapsed. I was in bad pain and very afraid. I only wanted to see Iman and Lexi again before the darkness came back and claimed me forever.

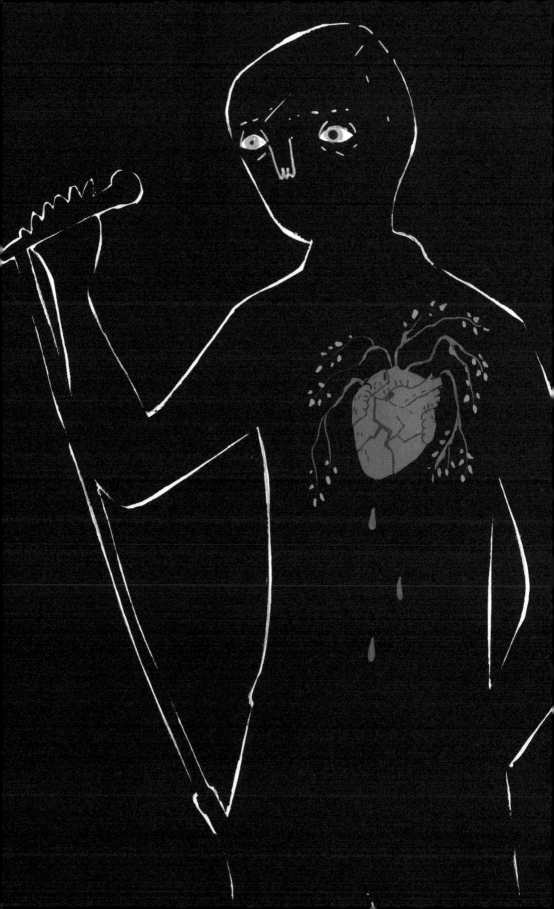

I CAN'T GIVE EVERYTHING AWAY

When I woke up after the operation, they told me I'd suffered a heart attack that almost killed me. It was time to concentrate on recovering my health.

I spent the following months walking in my city, reading, listening to music, and composing, but above all watching Lexi grow; I took her to the park like any other dad.

I was selective about the events I attended with Iman and decided to go only to performances that didn't threaten my health and that particularly intrigued me.

In September 2005 I returned to the stage to participate in Fashion Rocks, a fund-raiser for victims of Hurricane Katrina. Conscious of the audience's curiosity, I came out slowly, vulnerable, with an eye made up in black and a bandaged hand. My interpretation of "Life on Mars?" sounded very different than when it took me to stardom twenty-one years earlier: now it spoke of pain, mine and that of devastated Louisiana.

Although I didn't attend many of them, a number of events were held to recognize my career. While the world praised my work, I struggled to deal with my health problems. My faithful Iman got used to appearing alone at almost all our public commitments.

In 2006 I performed in public twice more: the first time, in London with David Gilmour at Albert Hall in a tribute to Syd Barrett, and the second time, with Alicia Keys to raise money for an AIDS prevention campaign for African children. I didn't realize these would be the last times I would go on stage.

At home, our life went on the same as ever. Our friends visited often. I kept composing, but without the pressure to release new records. Neither did I feel the vanity of previous years, the pressure to look perfect: I was closing in on sixty, and there was no point in trying to look eternally young. When I looked at myself in the mirror I recognized what I saw and accepted it. I had paid a high emotional price for the strain of reinventing myself throughout my life. Maybe my exit wouldn't be as triumphal as I'd dreamed, but I was content and at peace.

Nor did I forget the black cloud. It had returned to hide in the corners where the light couldn't reach. I knew that it was my keeper, and I became accustomed to its hidden presence.

My son, Duncan, was building his own career. His first feature film, *Moon*, premiered in 2009, and despite a low budget, it received very good reviews and won international prizes as well as one from the British Academy of Cinema and Television. We had in common a passion for science fiction. Duncan had talent, and I didn't want it to look like he was succeeding because he was my son. During the promotion I stayed on the sidelines, but I did attend the premiere with him at the Tribeca Film Festival in New York, and I was happy to be present at his moment of success. I had felt guilty in the past for neglecting my son, but now I saw that in the long run I hadn't exercised such a bad influence on him after all.

Little by little, the compositions piled up, solid material for an album. I got back together yet again with Tony Visconti. When we sat down again in the studio, Tony exclaimed, "This is going to be our *Sgt. Pepper!*" He said that every time we started a new record.

I called musicians I knew well: Zack Alford, Gail Ann Dorsey, Gerry Leonard. We signed a confidentiality pact: they were totally prohibited from telling anyone anything about the new project. They observed it faithfully; I knew I could trust them.

I got to the studio early, we started working, and at 6 p.m. I said to them that we'd finished for the day. At times the band was surprised to see me working in house slippers. So when *The Next Day* came out in March 2013, no one expected it. It got very good reviews, and the world was waiting for a new Bowie tour, but I wouldn't be ready until my heart recovered. I amused myself by recording an irreverent video for the title song with the actors Gary Oldman and Marion Cotillard, in which I appear as a messiah.

But my health kept getting worse, and in the summer of 2014 I was diagnosed with liver cancer. The dark haze was no longer hidden; it was everywhere. In spite of the fear and sadness that overtook me, I would face this last test looking forward.

I kept on writing and composing. Through the composer Maria Schneider I got to know Donny McCaslin, a brilliant jazz saxophonist, and his quartet. Like all the other times, I was enthusiastic about the musical challenge. It was the perfect format for the songs that surged from the fact of facing my existence with that growing black spot.

We recorded in the first months of 2015. The band was astonished when they saw me arrive without hair or eyebrows as a consequence of chemotherapy. I explained to them that I was ill and that no one should know. They gave me their word to keep it secret, and they complied. Visconti and I spent the following months giving these songs their definitive form.

There was one dream that hadn't yet come true: creating a musical. One night I went down to the basement of my house, where Thomas Jerome Newton still lurked, the alien I had brought to life in *The Man*

Who Fell to Earth. He hadn't changed: he was still young, sitting in front of the television and drinking. I said:

I DON'T KNOW IF I'LL BE HERE MUCH LONGER, SO I NEED YOU TO DO SOMETHING. YOU'RE GOING TO BE LAZARUS NOW. GET UP AND CONTINUE, FOR ME.

I pulled the creature out of the darkness, and in spite of my pain and fatigue, I worked to make the musical *Lazarus* become a reality. With much effort I attended the premiere, and it seemed to me like a success. I felt fortunate: my career had been full. It was November 2015.

From then on, the pain kept getting worse.

In January I turned sixty-nine. I was exhausted. I told Iman that the moment had come. We held hands tightly and the tears streamed down our faces.

While I was leaving planet Earth, my soul shredded as I heard my wife's inconsolable cry turn little by little into a distant echo.

I floated in complete silence. The black cloud, the most absolute darkness, came closer. I knew what it was: oblivion, the end of everything. An immense blackness that occupied the immensity of the cosmos. I was alone before it, an old man of almost seventy. But my identity had not disappeared, and the memories of my life overwhelmed me.

I saw myself as a child, playing in the streets of Bromley. I remembered the first time I heard the sound of my plastic saxophone. I listened attentively as Terry read aloud to me in our shared bedroom. I heard Duncan's first laugh, and Alexandria's. I saw again the look of gratitude on the faces of the fans at the end of a concert in 1972. I ran with my son in the African savannah. I laughed again at the crazy stories Iggy told us in Switzerland. The sensation on seeing Iman's gaze the first night we went out filled me with warmth. And the songs that I had listened to and created during my existence filled my soul.

My entire life condensed and burst into the form of an omnicolored flash that roared arrogantly at the shapeless mass. The stars of the cosmos reflected the cry and shone more intensely for an instant.

Then there was silence.

I took a step forward and calmly entered the darkness until it surrounded me completely.

I prepared to disappear into nothingness.

But there was something else there.

I looked forward and smiled.

BUT WHAT I SAW,
I WON'T REVEAL.

David Bowie (1967): Bowie's eponymous debut shows a twenty-year-old musician influenced by music-hall tradition and the theatricality of Anthony Newley and dazzled by all London has to offer.

David Bowie/Space Oddity (1969): A passion for Bob Dylan mixes with Bowie's first references to science fiction. "Cygnet Committee" suggests his disenchantment with hippie culture, and in "Letter to Hermione" Bowie opens his heart in a way that is unusual for him. The title single was his first big hit.

The Man Who Sold the World (1970): The unfolding of a personality, the Nietzchean superman, ambition, isolation: Bowie's great themes of the '70s resonate forcefully in his third LP.

Hunky Dory (1971): The first indispensable Bowie album focuses on piano-centered songs without abandoning the folk sensibility. Iconic numbers like "Changes" and "Life on Mars?" coexist with lesser-known jewels like "Quicksand" and "The Bewlay Brothers."

The Rise and Fall of Ziggy Stardust and the Spiders from Mars (1972): Kabuki theater, surrealism, science fiction, androgyny, and bisexuality—Bowie's most celebrated album demonstrates that full-on rock and roll could reflect previously marginalized sensibilities.

Aladdin Sane (1973): Bowie's glam-rock is enriched by the inclusion of avant-garde jazz pianist Mike Garson. Bowie presents new, strange, schizophrenic characters isolated amid desolate, irradiated landscapes.

Pin Ups (1973): A collection of '60s covers released at the moment of Bowie's peak fame, it sold well. The Bowie-Mick Ronson collaboration ends here.

Diamond Dogs (1974): Bowie definitively abandons glitter. In the era of oil shocks, this apocalyptic record was inspired by the writing of George Orwell.

Young Americans (1975): Bowie's passion for and great knowledge of black music explain the success of this project.

Station to Station (1976): Recorded when Bowie was headed for a crackup, its hallucinatory, enigmatic numbers jostle with other, more direct songs that he later described as a cry for help.

Low (1977): The first album of the "Berlin trilogy" is a declaration of intentions. Beneath its icy, experimental surface is the sound of a musician trying to heal his wounds.

"Heroes" (1977): The only album of the trilogy that was actually recorded entirely in Berlin, it is saturated with Bowie's impression of the city's tone. The title anthem was not a hit.

Lodger (1979): In spite of Brian Eno's touch and an avant-garde attitude, Bowie closed his trilogy with an incipient return to more conventional coordinates.

Scary Monsters . . . and Super Creeps (1980): New critical and commercial success arrives. Bowie contemplates his '70s output and proclaims his intention to bury it ("Ashes to Ashes") in order to let something new happen. In "Teenage Wildlife" he reflects on his place in the pop industry.

Let's Dance (1983): Sporting a new record deal, free at last from the yoke of Tony Defries, Bowie teamed up with Nile Rodgers to create a record that would make him rich. Its commerciality wasn't crass, and its hit singles have remained classics.

Tonight (1984): Bowie went into the studio to deliver a contractually obligated record. The absence of good ideas and of Nile Rodgers made for a record generally considered one of his lesser works. He included versions of Iggy Pop songs so that his broke friend could collect royalties.

Never Let Me Down (1987): The title song is a thank-you for his personal assistant Coco Schwab's years of loyalty. In spite of the spectacular tour that accompanied the album, Bowie here is a purely commercial artist who has run out of ideas.

Tin Machine (1989): To finish the decade, Bowie pulled off a move that surprised many: playing in a band of supposedly equal musicians. He explained that the project was based on simple chords that would permit the four artists room for improvisation and the possibility of expressing their own personalities.

Tin Machine II (1991): The quartet's second outing attracted little interest, and the project went no further. Nevertheless, guitarist Reeves Gabrels would continue working with Bowie in the following years.

Black Tie White Noise (1993): Though Bowie had dedicated most of the '80s to becoming wealthy, in the '90s his experimental spirit took over again. This new beginning includes the song he dedicated to Iman on the occasion of their wedding.

The Buddha of Suburbia (1993): The album, born out of Bowie's soundtrack for a BBC production, alternates accessible songs with some of his most experimental creations.

1.Outside (1995): A new collaboration with Brian Eno immersed Bowie in an avant-garde framework related to contemporary plastic arts. At the record's core is a reappearance of the idea of madness as a creative force.

Earthling (1997): Still on a quest not to become antiquated, Bowie gets on the drum-and-bass train. "Tell Lies" is a cryptic prophecy that looks at the change of millennium. "I'm Afraid of Americans" became a hit that seemed to reflect the feelings of many earthlings.

161

"hours . . ." (1999): Just before the beginning of the new century, Bowie, happy in real life, adopts a new disguise: the mature man facing midlife crisis. This was the first album by a major pop artist to be available by download on the internet.

Heathen (2002): Although the tone of this record was seemingly influenced by the 9/11 attacks, in reality it contains Bowie's reflections on the atheist culture that arose from Freud, Nietzsche, and Einstein.

Reality (2003): While on first listen this album seems more energetic than the previous one, at times it's equally melancholic. The world tour that followed its release was Bowie's last.

The Next Day (2013): In this surprise release after a long silence, Bowie appears for the first time outside of the system of release and promotion, in an album centered simply in his own restlessness.

★ **(Blackstar)** (2016): If in *Station to Station* Bowie confronts the abyss of madness, here he faces his own mortality. The result, in the words of his friend and producer Tony Visconti, shows "a man at the top of his game."

BIBLIOGRAPHY

Anderson, Sonia, dir. *Bowie: The Man Who Changed the World*. Screenbound, 2016.

Bowie, David. *Canciones I*. Translated by Alberto Manzano. Madrid: Fundamentos, 1998.

——. *Canciones II*. Translated by Alberto Manzano and Xavier Buendía. Madrid: Fundamentos, 1987.

——. Interview by Charlie Rose. *Charlie Rose*, March 31, 1998.

——. *VH1 Storytellers*. EMI, 2009.

Broackes, Victoria, and Geoffrey Marsh. *David Bowie Is Inside*. Barcelona: Malpaso, 2017.

Buckley, David. *Strange Fascination: David Bowie—The Definitive Story*. London: Random House, 2005.

Changes: Bowie at Fifty. BBC Two England documentary, 1997.

Critchley, Simon. *Bowie*. Madrid: Sexto Piso, 2016.

David Bowie: Five Years. BBC documentary, 2013.

Hewitt, Paolo. *Bowie*. Barcelona: Blume, 2016.

O'Leary, Chris. "Pushing Ahead of the Dame." Blog, https://bowiesongs.wordpress.com.

Sandford, Christopher. *Amando al extraterrestre*. Madrid: T&B, 2016.

Trynka, Paul. *Starman: La biografía definitiva*. Barcelona: Alba, 2016.

Whately, Francis, dir. *David Bowie: The Last Five Years*. BBC, 2017.

Yentob, Alan, dir. *Cracked Actor: A Film about David Bowie*. BBC, 1975.

ACKNOWLEDGMENTS

To Mireia, who as my editor has cared for me like a friend, a sister, and a mother.

To Cristina G., Fran R., Ana C., Noemí A., Javi J., Lucía A., Miguel J., Jesús B., and Raquel E., friends who are always there, who have put up with my weeping and wailing, who have energized me and always have believed in me. Who keep my feet on the ground.

To Laura Agustí and Rebeca Khamlichi, with whom I have shared the gestation and birth of this book. What luck to have you there to unwind with. I always learn from you.

To Alfonso, who keeps taking me by the hand and moving me forward.

To Fran, the author of the text of this book, for teaching me to love David Robert Haywood Jones. And for the affection that went into the creation of this book.

To my mom: I'll always be grateful to you, there's no one who believes in me more than you.

—MARÍA HESSE

To Blanca Ladrón, for reminding me that writing a book is something to enjoy.

To Cristina Ladrón, Iñaki Pérez, and Antonio Berrocal, for advice and so much laughter with *Stranger Things* on in the background.

To Guillermo Laín Corona, for helping me with the mechanics of the Spanish language. And for all the rest.

To Carmen Sales Delgado, for advising me on the translation.

To María Hesse, illustrator and cat lover, for deciding that I was the right person to put on the David Bowie disguise.

To my family, for embracing an alien in their midst. And for the infinite patience they have with him.

To Marta, for improving the text with her suggestions. And for making me better.

—FRAN RUIZ

To Lola Martínez de Albornoz, for her heroic editing job. And for surviving together with us the madness that permeates everything connected with Bowie.

To David Robert Haywood Jones, for carrying us beyond the rainbow.

—MARÍA HESSE AND FRAN RUIZ